Wake Up Bitch
And Fix Me Some Chicken

Crazy People Say The Darnest Things

Wake Up Bitch

And Fix Me Some Chicken

Crazy People Say The Darnest Things

true stories from the nut house by

John R. Booth

Wake Up Bitch And Fix Me Some Chicken:
Crazy People Say The Darnest Things

ISBN-10: 0985810378
ISBN-13: 978-0-9858103-7-5

Freeze Time Media

Cover illustration by Di Freeze
Chicken Illustration by Memo Angeles

This book is dedicated to all my crazy patients and the woman I am crazy about, my wife, Becca.

Acknowledgments

First, I must give a big thanks to my wife who, for more years than she thought she bargained for, has endured my presence and that of the patients I brought home in my mind. She encouraged me to continue when mental acuity was impeded by brain lock and knew when departure from writing was the cure: "Honey, I know you can find the right word eventually, but right now, fuck it, go play some golf." I love that girl.

Next, my children and grandchildren, who kept the memories alive by having me tell and retell the cleaned-up versions of these stories. Thank you, Lindy G., for making it impossible to not write this book by telling everyone I was writing it before I had put one word to the page. Thanks to my mother for encouraging me to get into social work (I would have thought she would have wanted better for her oldest son), and thanks to all who I worked with … too many to name but you know who you are: the nurses, doctors, social workers, administrators, housekeepers, security staff, charge aides, primary care aides, maintenance crew, medical records staff, pharmacy crew, IT guys, administrative assistants and psychologists — even the one who treated most of us like shit.

Thank you, Di Freeze. I had nothing but words on a page, and you turned them into a book. Don't ever let anyone blame you for the content. That's on me.

Most of all: God bless my former patients. They are some of the most precious people on earth. Anybody who has ever worked with mentally ill patients and says they loved them all is a liar. Some of my patients weren't even likable, let alone loveable. But they were all precious. Not one of them ever asked to be mentally ill. At one time they were all somebody's baby child, with parents who wanted nothing but the best in life for them. Not one of them ever told me that they woke up one day and decided, "Yeah, crazy. That's the ticket. If I could just be a burden to my family. If I could just strain their nerves, finances, and love until it has all run out. If I could live under a bridge, get arrested and put in jail, spend most of my life scared shitless, guess at reality, and guess wrong most of the time, expose myself to unspeakable diseases, self-medicate with alcohol, be beaten up regularly, be taken advantage of routinely, teased for just being me, live with unrequited love, and have no understanding of how it all happened. Yeah, crazy, that would be my heart's desire." Most endured. Some found it too painful and ended the suffering. All will live in my heart.

Contents

Foreword

Writing a book is difficult and humbling. It makes you doubt if you were ever really funny, creative, clever or even literate. So:

To all who bought this book, I apologize. I am not, nor have I ever aspired to be, a writer. Family and friends goaded me into writing this collection of anecdotal remembrances as a social worker at the oldest mental health facility in our state, and later, at the only forensic mental health center in our state. I would entertain these friends and family members with stories of funny things my patients had said or done. They insisted that if I should ever write a book containing these tales, everyone would buy a copy. (I intend to hold them to that.)

What I found immediately upon initiating this literary endeavor was that it is much easier to tell a funny story than it is to write a funny story. An oral accounting of an event is punctuated and heightened with vocal inflections and physical interpretations, which add emotion and character to the telling. When I would put the same story down on paper, it would just lay there, sounding to me like a monotone collection of vaguely related words sans interest or readability. I wrote and rewrote every line. I obsessed over the characters and spent hours debating every verb and adjective. After months of stuttered starts, flurries of penned sewage, and prodigious amounts of self-inflicted dubiety, I finally decided "Fuck 'em. None of them are now or ever will write a book. At least I'm trying. If they don't like my book, tough shit. They still have to buy it. They promised!"

But to you, the anonymous, the unsuspecting yet very much appreciated few who bought this book believing that it would be a good read, I apologize.

No refunds!

But, I do apologize.

Cast of Characters

Before you read this book, it is important that you know the cast of world-class characters that I had the privilege to work with every day. Most of the people listed below are actual staff members I got to work with; however, some are an amalgam, based on two or more people, blending their most remarkable, best, and in some cases worst, traits. All the people are real. All the names are fake. The patients (with all of their names changed) are all true, and no blending of characteristics or traits has been attempted. They are unusual enough by themselves. All the stories are true.

John Booth: That's me. I was a social worker at both the state mental hospital and the forensic mental hospital that it morphed into. I am five feet ten inches tall with my boots on. My body weight is within societal norms. I have been told that I am okay looking, for an older guy with no hair on top. My position as a social worker, and my role in the treatment of the patients was less than glamorous, and varied little from day to day. I will offer no psychobabble of the value I brought to the patients, their families, or the community. To be honest, I could have trained a motivated monkey do to my job in about two weeks. My primary function was to keep families off the doctors' back. In doing that, I learned to eat little bits of shit from them and the patients daily, and over the course of my career, I learned to do it without gagging. When not doing that, I was a member of the treatment team that developed individualized treatment and discharge plans for the patients. For most of my career, at any given time, I had about thirty patients to deal with. The last four years of my career, due to understaffing, I had from seventy-five to one hundred patients on three different units, on two different pods, and on opposite ends of the hospital.

Nurse Kiki was the head nurse on the admission unit I was assigned to. She was in her early to mid-twenties, five feet two inches tall, perfect skin, perfect teeth, perfect body, could and would cuss like a sailor, and was fucking HOT. She was the head of the unit, and when all was said and done, she was responsible for everything that happened on her unit while she was there. She knew mental health inside and out, was respectful but firm with the patients, exceedingly fair with her staff, and did I mention, she's fucking HOT. Doctor Shrinkwrap said, on more than one occasion, "Nurse Kiki really messes with my head. She's so young that I feel a paternal protectiveness toward her, and want to ravage her all at the same time. Does that make me fucked up?" Yes. Yes it does.

Doctor Enrico Shrinkwrap was the psychiatrist on the units. He was in his late sixties and handsome in that way that older Italian men get when they age (think Dean Martin). He was one of the finest mental health care professionals I ever worked with. He was kind to a fault, unpretentious, respectful to his patients(to their face), funny as hell, and a hoot to work with. He got his training primarily in some Central American country with a name like something out of a Woody Allen movie. Contrabananastan, or something like that. I have never been able to find it on a map.

Stiffany was the charge aide on the unit. Her name was the combination of Stephanie and Tiffany. I don't know why, other than maybe it settled some naming rights argument between her parents. Of course, behind her back Dr. Shrinkwrap called her Stiffenme. She was in her thirties, but looked younger. Long blonde hair, a classically beautiful face, five feet ten inches or so tall, and mammarily blessed, or as one of the patients said once, "She has very big breastesess." She was "second in command" on the unit, being in charge of and directing the primary care aides (PCAs) in their handling of the day-to-day care of the patients. I have never met a person who was better than her at cutting through the bullshit of a situation and developing/implementing a solution.

Captain Headlock was the chief security officer. He was, obviously, in charge of the five or six security officers we had on any given shift at the hospital. He was ex-Marine, ex-cop, ex-husband of two of the nurses at the hospital, and exceedingly proud of himself and his performance of his duties. Being ex-Marine and ex- cop, and being a bodybuilding freak, he had freakishly large muscles. Six feet tall with five percent body fat, buzz-cut hair, never passed a mirror or his reflection in a window that he didn't give a little pectoral flex to, wore clothes that looked a little too tight, and luckily, he seemed to like me.

Doctor Corkscrew was the president of the medical staff. His claim to fame was his longevity. He had managed to stay on staff at both the old and the new hospitals for a total of thirty-three years. Bravo. He was a really nice guy, always showed up at least an hour after everyone else, and in all situations took the path of least resistance.

Doctor Smellyme was a foreign-born and educated young doctor. He claimed to have done work in Boston at Mass General Hospital, but nobody ever cared or took the time to verify this claim. Our hospital was his first job away from an academic setting. He was convinced that he was the smartest person in any room he walked into and was not bashful to tell you that he was the smartest person there.

Glossary of Terms

Treatment Team: The psychiatrist, registered nurse, and social worker. The task of the treatment team was to develop an individualized treatment plan for each patient and monitor the patient's progress toward discharge criteria.

Charge Nurse: The registered nurse in charge of any given unit. Hell, who am I kidding; they ran the whole hospital.

Med. Nurse: A licensed practical nurse (LPN) who administered daily medications to the patients. Warning: don't ever come up to an LPN and ask her/him where the nurse is. They will be quick to point out that they have a license that says "nurse" just like a registered nurse. I found it was a best practice to stay on the good side of anyone who had "license" or "nurse" in their title.

Charge Aide: The charge aide was normally a non-degreed person who was the ramrod for all primary care aides on any given unit. They either 1) had been around and had a world of experience; 2) were a cut above, more organized, more respected by patients and staff; or 3) had done an admirable job of sucking up to move out of the ranks of the PCA. My experience with charge aides indicated that it was most often a case of 1 and 2.

PCA (Primary Care Aide): The PCA was the person

who did most of the work on the unit. My respect for them is incalculable. The PCA was always face to face with the patients, the first one who ran toward trouble, the first one to defuse a potentially bad situation, the first one called on to do any dirty work, and the first one blamed for anything that went wrong. On a daily basis, they were subjected to all manner of verbal and physical abuse at the hands of patients (spit on, shit and piss thrown on them, they and their families called everything in the book, bones broken, faces battered and bloodied, food thrown on them, etc.). They have saved my ass numerous times, and they will always have my gratitude and respect.

DSM: Diagnostic and Statistics Manuel

CTP: Comprehensive Treatment Plan

Revolving door patient: a patient who is in and out of the hospital regularly, usually due to noncompliance with prescribed medication.

SHPOS (Sub Human Piece Of Shit): pronounced schpoze, a diagnosis, first explained to me by Nurse Kiki, given to the most disgusting patients or to patients who had committed the most horrible crimes.

GAS level (Give A Shit level): I think this is self-explanatory.

AMF (Adios Mother Fucker): Staff sentiment expressed whenever a particularly disgusting patient was returned to county jail. Example: "Hey Jake, where is that SHPOS Mr. Carpenter?" "He's AMF."

Bush Therapy: Sex between two consenting patients usually done outside behind a bush or clump of trees. The same term is applied to any surreptitious sex between patients regardless of location.

Introduction

Before I start the disjointed ramblings between the covers of this book, I feel the need to give the reader some background information. Once I get past this task, the remainder will be a collection of anecdotal recollections about the patients and the time I spent at the "nut house."

It was in the mid 1980s, and I was between wives and between jobs when I was hired as a social worker. Not just a garden-variety social worker, but a social worker at the "nut house," a state-operated mental health hospital in a South Central state of the United States. By the time I got there, the hospital was almost one hundred years old. Almost all structures were two-, three- and four-story red brick buildings with red tile roofs, situated on a multi-acre plot of ground in the northeast corner of the state. When I say the northeast corner of the state, I mean in the middle of nowhere. The nearest town is about two miles away, with a population of about five thousand souls, one third of which, for whatever reason, do not have a high school education.

The hospital sat at the top of a windswept hill, with the red brick buildings separated by large, grassy lawns dotted with catalpa, oak, elm, cedar and fir trees. At one time the hospital was completely self-sufficient. It had its own power house, water supply, cattle ranch, vegetable farm, and fire department. Also on the grounds was a clinic/hospital unit to treat other than mental health maladies, a bank, a baseball field complete with concession stand, a gymnasium, a beauty parlor/barbershop, a library, a canteen that made the best hamburgers anywhere (it was rumored that this was because the griddle had never been cleaned), it's own newspaper, a church, a morgue, and a cemetery. It was completed with a dormitory for staff to live in, single-family houses for the doctors, and the "Big House" for the superintendent to live in.

At the height of its utilization, the hospital housed around three thousand patients. The first patients were brought in by train and deposited just outside of town. Those that could walk went the rest of the way on foot, with the others taken by whatever transportation was available. This was a time before the development of psychotropic medications, so treatment was limited to hydrotherapy, electroconvulsive therapy, and the like. Many of the patients worked on the cattle ranch and the vegetable farm. Because of the limited therapies available, most patients at that time stayed for years and years, with many spending most of their lives there. It sounds sad to think of someone being admitted to the "nut house" and never being allowed to leave. However, if you could find any of the "old-timers," they would tell you that it was home to them and that they were happy there.

By the time I went to work there in the late 1980s, the population had been reduced to about three hundred patients, and most staff lived off of the property in town. It was at about this time that the national trend was to downsize or totally do away with state-run mental health facilities. In response to this, and by state mandate, the population continued to be brought down until the old facility was no longer necessary.

A new facility was built on adjacent acreage, but with a new mission. It was no longer the state hospital for the mentally ill, but instead was the state forensic center for mentally ill patients. The population was made up of individuals who had been accused of crimes and were found to be incompetent to stand trial. They were court ordered to this facility to undergo treatment to restore them to competency so they could return to the county jail and eventually go to trial for their alleged crimes. It also became the facility to house all criminals who were deemed to be "Not Guilty By Reason of Insanity" (NGRI). I call them criminals instead of patients because to be deemed NGRI, the person had to admit to having done the crime but prove that they were unable to distinguish right from wrong at the moment they committed the crime. All were guilty as hell, and most were crazy has hell.

I loved working under the old system in the old facility, and I loved working in the new facility under the new mission. I met a lot of patients who were treated, discharged, and never returned. I met a lot of "revolving door" patients who never seemed to be able to function outside of the hospital. I met one patient who was born at the state mental hospital and died at the same state hospital. The stories that follow were taken from my experiences at both facilities. Most of the stories, to me, are funny as hell because mentally ill people are, to me, funny as hell. One or two stories are sad because — well, that's the way life is sometimes.

I remember my first day at the hospital just like it was yesterday, primarily because of the first person I met. As I turned off the highway onto the blacktop county road that led to the hospital, I drove past a sign that warned, "Hitchhikers may be escaped patients." I thought to myself, "What the fuck have I gotten into? Just how dangerous are these folks? Would I be a real pussy to turn around?" I didn't know the answer to the first two questions, but the answer to the last question would be, "Yes, I would be a big pussy if I didn't at least show up."

I drove on for two miles on the blacktop road and came to a stone entrance with a sign that welcomed all visitors and directed them to check in at the administration building. I was a little early on that day, so I drove around the grounds to take a look-see. I took a right-hand turn and followed the road that went past what appeared to be some sort of patient housing. About one hundred yards around the corner past the gate, I saw people just wandering around on what looked a lot like a college campus. I found out later that the folks roaming around were patients, but none looked like what I imagined a "crazy person" would look like. I mean, I had seen "One Flew Over The Cuckoo's Nest," "Halloween," "Harvey," etc., and in all those movies the patients were locked up and wore nothing but nightgowns. These patients were dressed in blue jeans, shirts, tennis shoes, and for the most part didn't appear "crazy."

I didn't know at that time that these were the "best of the best" and that, most assuredly, there were Cuckooesque patients locked up behind the doors of the buildings I was passing by. I pulled my car over to a shaded parking spot, got out, and leaned against the front fender. I had not been there but two minutes when a large black lady came walking past. She had her arms spread wide, as if herding chickens, and was saying, "Come on now. You children stay together. Don't make me have to get after you in front of this nice man here."

I seriously looked around trying to find the children she was talking to, until it dawned on me that she was hallucinating, and that she was the only one who could see or hear those children. Following her was a tall, thin, bearded guy who shuffled by, repeatedly chanting, "Poodle bite, poodle bite, poodle bite."

Farther away, I could see a younger man gamboling cross the lawn, running, leaping, and raising his arms in what appeared to be a display of uninhibited celebration of a sunny, warm morning. Closer inspection revealed that he was chasing, catching, and eating defenseless monarch butterflies that were migrating across the state.

At that point I decided I should find my office. In route I had to pass by a hedge. Nearing it, I heard what I at first interpreted as a female in distress. I turned the corner at the end of the hedge row and found a male and female patient, naked bodies entwined and engaged in what I later learned was called "Bush Therapy." And these were the "good ones" who had the freedom to walk about outside without an escort or supervision — Holy Crap!

Welcome to your new career, John.

Dan

Ours was the only forensic mental health facility in a state of seventy-seven counties, and our forensic facility only had two hundred beds. Of those two hundred beds, seventy-five or so were permanently occupied at any given time by patients who were deemed by the court to be NGRI (Not Guilty By Reason of Insanity). I always thought that NGRI was bullshit. Those patients were far from not guilty.

To use the NGRI plea, the defendant has to admit that they did the crime but that they did not know right from wrong at the specific moment they committed the act. Now I ask you, how can someone admit to committing a crime and be not guilty of that crime at the same time? I always thought the plea should be Guilty But Insane. But that is just my opinion and is better left for another time.

I said all that to say this. I was in the admissions area of the forensic hospital. Sitting across the desk from Doctor Shrinkwrap, Nurse Kiki, and me was an old black gentleman named Dan who absolutely looked like he had been sitting in a small town county jail for eighteen months. You could immediately tell that he was malnourished.

Side note: It was not unusual for these patients to lose weight while in jail. Once the other inmates of the county jail found out that these guys were crazy,

1

they would start to take advantage of them. Sometimes they would put disgusting things in the crazy guy's food (piss, shit, snot, semen, etc.), causing the crazy inmate to refuse to eat. More often, however, the other inmates would intimidate the crazy inmate into giving his food to them. I was always amazed that the jailers either didn't see this going on or didn't ever seem to do anything about it if they did see it going on.

A tray of food was ordered for Dan. It was standard fare for the hospital: mystery meat loaf, mashed potatoes, small green salad with tomatoes and French dressing, red Jell-O, coffee, tea, one slice of white bread, and yellow cake with chocolate icing. Dan began devouring this meal with the kind of gusto and appreciation usually only seen in World War Two news reels of reclaimed prisoners of war. Instead of being in the orange jailhouse jumpsuit that most prisoners wore when they were brought to us, this poor soul was wearing the clothes he had been arrested in: dirty cotton dress pants and cotton work shirt that hung on him like they were five sizes too large. Tennis shoes that had exceeded the expiration date completed his incarceration ensemble. The clothes pretty much smelled like they had never been washed.

He had also grown a beard while in custody. This was probably because he had been refused a razor once it was determined that he was crazy. His teeth looked like they hadn't seen a toothbrush for the duration of his incarceration, and his breath validated this assumption. Dirt — at least I hoped it was dirt — was caked under fingernails that were about one and a half inches long. Despite his rumpled and filthy exterior, he was surprisingly articulate for one of our patients. He spoke in measured tones in a voice that reminded me of that black guy on TV that sells insurance. He was courteous and respectful in his responses to questions and did not give the impression that he was responding to internal stimuli (hallucinations).

Doctor Shrinkwrap started the admission interview with the usual questions.

"How old are you?"

"I'll be sixty-six my next birthday, so I guess that makes me sixty-five," Dan replied after swallowing a mouthful of mashed potatoes.

"Man, you could have fooled me," Doctor Shrinkwrap said as he raised his eyebrows. "I thought you were at least seventy-five or eighty. Mental illness is a sumbitch. It has worked your ass over but good."

"Yes, sir, it has," Dan answered respectfully. "What with being crazy and in and out of jail most of my adult life, I haven't had the inclination to take very good care of myself. I apologize for my appearance."

"Geez, fella, you said a mouthful, and I don't mean mashed potatoes. You are right. The crazy life has worked your ass over but good."

Doctor Shrinkwrap could be so compassionate at times.

"When is your birthday, fella? Doctor Shrinkwrap asked, with pen in hand, ready to fill out the all-important paperwork.

"November eighteenth," Dan mumbled as he ate.

"November eighteenth. Okay, what year?"

Dan looked up from his meal.

"Every year," he said with a mischievous smile.

Doctor Shrinkwrap and Nurse Kiki had an interview/interrogation routine that I had endured a thousand times. I was about to fall asleep.

Doctor Shrinkwrap, for some reason, would ask

the same question three or four times, pissing the patient off.

"Dan, do you hear voices."

"No."

"Have you ever heard things that no one else heard, like voices?"

"I said no."

"When was the last time you heard someone talking and there was no one there?"

"What?"

"Dan, are you responding to voices right now?"

"Doc, do you not understand English? I've answered the same questions four times by my count. Can we either move on, take me to my cell, or send me back to jail? You are making me fucking crazy and mad as hell. I was trying to like you, but you're starting to be an asshole. Do you not hear my answers, not like my answers, or are you just being a prick?"

Nurse Kiki, as if it were scripted, would verbally step in and smooth things over, giving the patient some longwinded bullshit reason for the preceding question fest.

"Dan, what the doctor is trying to determine, establish, document, and codify is your current ability, based on your perception of past life experiences, to listen, comprehend, assimilate, collate, and filterate repeated auditory stimuli into a cogent, goal-directed, meaningful dialogue in real time, and thus build the foundation for an appropriate diagnostification."

"Uh, what? Oh, okay. Since you've explained it, I guess it's okay. I'm sorry I blew up like that, Doc."

Doctor Shrinkwrap, having been bailed out and vindicated by Nurse Kiki, would begin again.

"How long have you been depressed?"

"I'm not depressed."

"I mean, you know, depressed, sad, blue, feeling down, shit like that."

"I'm not depressed."

"When you get this way, how long does it last — a few days, a few weeks? After this depression lasts for a while, are you suicidal, wanna kill yourself, call it quits, eat a bullet sandwich, take a long walk off a short pier, kick the bucket, take a dirt nap, check it all in, take the fast lane to the big kahuna? Do you wanna die, big fella?"

"Nurse, he's doing it again."

This went on and on for what seemed like an hour. Doctor Shrinkwrap pushed back from the desk, gave a nod to Dan, and whispered to Nurse Kiki, "I'm done here. I think I've got a pretty good handle on this nut case. You want to go fool around?"

Nurse Kiki was about ninety-two percent sure that Doctor Shrinkwrap was not serious about fooling around, this also being part of their routine. She took a breath and told Dan, "We are almost done. I think John has just a few questions for you."

"Okay."

Upon meeting a new patient, I always wanted to find out if they knew where they were and why they were here.

"Dan, do you know where you are right now?" I began.

"I guess I'm at some sort of nut house," he replied. "However, in all the nut houses I have ever been to, this is the first one that was surrounded by barbed wire. Just how dangerous do you think I am?"

I shrugged. "I'm just now meeting you, so I don't have any idea how dangerous you are." I then went on the explain to him, "You are at the state forensic hospital."

"Forensic hospital — what does that mean?" he asked.

"A forensic mental health hospital — nut house — treats patients who have been accused of a crime but have also been found to not be competent to stand trial," I replied. "Our patients are of varying degrees of dangerousness. Some are murderers and some are just shoplifters. All of them must have their mental illness stabilized. Once stabilized, education can start and competency restoration established."

I then asked, "Now that you know what kind of a nut house you are in, do you know why you were brought here? Do you know what you have been charged with?"

"No, sir, I don't."

I think to myself: *Unbelievable. If I had been in jail for eighteen minutes, I would want to know why I was there, but this guy was in jail for eighteen months, and it didn't dawn on him at any time to ask someone why he was there.*

What I say out loud is, "Well, sir, you have several charges against you right now. Would you like to know what they are?"

"Yes, sir, I would."

I open my notebook and read his charges.

"Dan, you have been charged with indecent exposure, forcible oral sodomy, and kidnapping."

"I don't know what any of that means. I know I had been with a lady friend of mine that evening, and later the police came and arrested me. But I don't know what those charges mean?"

Dan seemed to legitimately be in distress about

being charged with a crime. This was clearly the first time he recognized that he was in trouble. His voice quivered a little, and his eyes looked scared and got blood shot, like he was trying not to cry.

"What does that mean?" he asked again, a painful quality in his voice.

I opened up the file of legal paperwork that had been given to me prior to his arrival.

"Let's look at your police report and see what it has to say. It says here that you were indeed with a lady. They say you invited her to your apartment, and that while she was in your apartment you unfastened your pants and pulled out your penis. That would be the indecent exposure charge. It also says in the police report that you forced her to put your penis into her mouth and leave it there until you ejaculated. That would be the forcible oral sodomy. Then, it goes on to state that when that was over you made her drink wine with you and wouldn't let her leave. That would be the kidnapping charge. Do you understand now?"

"I understand the words you are saying, and it sounds like I am in trouble, but how would the police know all that happened if the lady and I were the only two people in my apartment?"

"That is a very good question," I answered. "What happened was, the lady you were with must have gone to the police, told them what happened, and pressed charges against you. Blah, blah, blah, long story short, here you are."

"I just don't get it," Dan said, shaking his head in disbelief. "I just don't get it."

"What don't you get?" I asked as I started turning back to the front of his folder. "Do you want me to go over it again?"

"No, you don't have to go over all that stuff again. I understand the charges and all, but I just don't get it."

"What?"

"I don't get how I could be in trouble. I did all that stuff they said I did. But, Mr. John, I can't be in trouble, because that's the way I does all my women."

That's the way he does all his women? Holy shit.

Doug the Firebug

Another day at the funny farm, and Doctor Shrink-wrap, Nurse Kiki, and I were back in admissions, this time to meet Doug the Firebug. Doug was coming to us from a very rural county in the southernmost part of our state. From looking at his file, it was a garden-variety case of "Attempting to Manufacture and Distribute Methamphetamines" with a "Second Degree Arson" tacked on for good measure.

According to the police report, the fire department was called out to a house fire. Upon extinguishing the blaze, they found the remains of what appeared to be a meth lab. Doug was arrested and taken to jail. With his means of making a living "up in smoke," Doug could not afford an attorney, so he was given a court-appointed attorney. A public defender, or as he put it, a "public pretender."

I had read all his paperwork: the arrest report, the report to the court made by the public defender, and the report issued by the psychologist who was called in when it was believed that he was too crazy to get a fair trial. The treatment team, and for that matter, the entire staff, had what Stiffany the charge aide called "a highly sensitive shitometer, capable of sorting out a bat shit crazy patient from a bullshit malingering patient." I wasn't sure yet where Doug the Firebug fell on the shitometric scale, but my gut told me he was high on the bullshit end of the spectrum. But I could be wrong. I had been before.

Doug the Firebug was a stereotypical redneck male from the rural south end of the state. He was about five feet nine inches tall, muscular, tattooed up, wore his hair in a mullet, had a wife that went by two names (Barbie Jean), and was convinced that he was smarter than "all the fucking cops in the state." Doug the Firebug had stretch marks on his chest and biceps.

"I got them there scars from lifting weights while I was in prison," said the guy who believed he was smarter than "all the fucking cops in the state," pointing to each one individually with his best redneck smirk, and without prompting. (Yeah, smarter than all the cops.) "We was lifting weights. I could bench about five hundred fifty pounds, and I got them stretch marks when my muscles got too damn big." (My ass.)

Doctor Shrinkwrap and Nurse Kiki began their song and dance routine with Doctor Shrinkwrap pissing the patient off several times and Nurse Kiki trying to make it all better with sweet psychobabble. It has been my experience that most people who are legitimately mentally ill do not advertise it, do not brag about it, and try their best to keep it hidden. Doug the Firebug was no exception. He denied a need for mental health treatment; however, his paranoia was on display for all to see and hear. Here is the story as Doug the Firebug told it to Doctor Shrinkwrap, Nurse Kiki, and me.

"That damn county sheriff and his deputies had been tryin' to get my ass ever since I got out of prison."

"Oh, really. What were you in prison for?"

"They say I was manufacturing and sellin' meth. That's all bullshit, and you can ask anybody I know.

I'm an honest, law-abiding guy. Really. Anyhow, they was all the time stoppin' me for bullshit stuff, but they could never make any of it stick. I kinda think they were tryin' to get me to leave the county, 'cause that's what the sheriff's deputy told me once during a traffic stop — that they were going to fuck with me until I left the county. I wasn't goin' nowhere. I grew up in this county, and they can't make me leave. Fuck 'em. Anyways, when they couldn't get nothing to stick by stopping me all the time, they started following me around. They were pretty good, 'cause I couldn't see them doin' it most of the time, but I knew they was there. They was followin' my wife and kids around too. Now, that's just not right. I coulda sued them for that if I wanted to, but then they woulda knowd I was on to 'em and their scheme. So, when they couldn't get me that way they hired some guys from out of the county — state guys — to spy on me in my home."

"You mean that they stationed people in your neighborhood to spy on you? Keep track of your comings and goings — stuff like that? Did they do like a stakeout across from your house?" I asked.

"No. They put guys in my house to spy on me." WTF. " I can prove it. Little midgets in the walls and in my attic. I could hear them running around at night, and sometimes during the day if I was real quiet. That's the way those little prick-ass midget fuckers are. I know they were state guys 'cause the county don't hire no midget fuckers. Never have. Never will. I tried stayin' up all day and all night to catch the little bastards, but they wouldn't come out when I was awake. They would just look at me through holes in the walls. I could only do that — stay up — for three or four days at a time. One time it was almost a week, but I had some pharmaceutical help to stay up that time.

"Anyways, when I couldn't catch them myself, I set up traps around the house to catch 'em. Some were like bear traps that would've snapped the little spyin' bastards in half if it caught 'em. Some of them were little, minor-explosive devices with trip wires that would have blown their asses up a little bit, but those little prick-ass midget fuckers were damn smart. I didn't catch or blow up one damn midget. Then I got real smart. I put up one of those cameras that hunters use to find deer and shit. You know, one of those cameras they tie to a tree, and it takes pictures at night when something moves. I put up one of those and, bam, I caught the little prick-ass midget fucker bastards on film. Now that I had proof that I had 'em but couldn't catch 'em, I was stumped about what to do.

"Then, one night it come to me. I could just burn the assholes out. Problem solved. So, I sent the wife and kids away for the weekend. No sense gettin' them in the line of fire, so to speak. When they were gone, I spread a bunch of gasoline and kerosene and paper and stuff around the house and set it on fire. I was gonna have me some bar-b-qued prick-ass midget fuckers. Then the fire department came, and the police came, and I got thrown in the pokey on trumped-up charges."

Whew, no paranoia here. Nothing to see, just keep moving folks.

"I tried to tell my public pretender about it, but he didn't believe me and thought I was crazy. He asked the court to have me tested. The judge pulled in some pencil-necked geek that called hisself a psychologist. That asshole spent an hour with me before he was done and left. It was him that I guess had the final say-so and called me officially crazy, but I'm telling you, those little prick-ass midget fuckers were there, and I got proof. Until I accidentally burned it up with the house."

I think to myself, *Really, it took him a full hour to figure out you were nuts? I've been with nut boy here for fifteen minutes and have him diagnosed as loony toons.*

"Thanks for the explanation. I'm done here. One of the security officers will take you to the unit."

My next step, typically, was to contact the patient's family to let them know their loved one was no longer in jail, and that he was with us and was all right. I also would interview the next of kin to obtain background information, sociological data, and cultural data. In this case I called Doug the Firebug's wife, Barbie Jean. She was very helpful and grateful that Doug the Firebug was with us. I always ended my phone interview by asking if they had any questions.

"Yes, sir, I do. How long do you think Dougie will be with y'all?" she asked in a cute, babyish voice that I am sure had disarmed many a poor sucker and had persuaded more than one state troopers to forego issuing a traffic citation. "Since he burned all the stuff up — I mean, burned the house down — we ain't got no way to earn a living."

"Barbie Jean," I said, "I don't have an answer to that. All I can tell you is that since he was accused of a felony crime, by statute we can work with him for up to two years to restore competency. "

"Shit," Barbie Jean whimpered.

"Barbie Jean, can I ask you one more question?"

"Why, sure you can, hon," she said with a sniffle.

"Well, Barbie Jean, what can you tell me about the midgets?"

Her voice perked up, and she said, "If I hadn't seen em' with my own eyes, I wouldn't have believed it."

Hmmmm. A shared delusion or a shared crack pipe? Coin toss.

Eldon

As is my usual morning routine, I rang the buzzer to enter the hospital. Upon entering, I took a hard right turn to the employees break room. After I swiped my name badge to gain entry, I heard the lock click open and I went in. The break room had four or five square tables that would seat four people each. Each table had salt pepper and napkins centered on them. Three vending machines were behind the tables: one for cookies, candy, etc.; one for sandwiches, burritos, etc.; and the last for soda, bottled water, and tea. To the immediate left of this area was an area with rows of lockers for the staff to stow coats, lunch, phones, and the like. Everything other than what you were wearing was supposed to stay in your locker, and everyone was very careful to abide by this rule (wink, wink).

I went to my locker, twisted the dial that turned the tumblers, and unlocked my one-foot by one-foot by three-foot coat receptacle. I dumped my jacket, slammed it shut, and headed out to my office. Just outside the break room door was the reception desk. To the left of that was the entrance to the patient areas of the hospital. To enter there you have to pass through a metal detector and wait to be buzzed through by security. Literally every person that passed through activated a loud and obnoxious alarm on the metal detector. No one was ever searched or patted down to see what had set the alarm off, and everyone was always buzzed through. Anyone could have passed through there with a hunting knife in their pocket, a 9mm handgun in the waistband of their pants, and a shotgun strapped under their pant leg. I have no idea why the damn thing was there.

I passed through this and the attached sally port in route to the bowels of the hospital, where all of the real work took place. On this day I decided to forgo going to my office and instead headed straight to one of my admission units. I swiped my badge over the electronic lock, and with the accompanying click was allowed entry. I walked down a short hall, past the treatment room, and past the laundry room with blue bags of dirty laundry piled outside. I put a smile on my face and pushed through the door to the nurse's station.

"Hey, kids, who we gonna fix today?" I asked, truly in a good mood that morning.

Stiffeny fixed me with a stare that I had grown to simultaneously love and fear and said, "They're all too broke to be fixed, and one of the brokenest ones wants to see you ASAP."

"Yippee," I chirped, feigning enthusiasm. "Would ya give me a hint? As far as I can tell, they're all pretty messed up."

Her gaze never altered, except to give a quick nod in the direction of Eldon, a twenty-something male of mixed parentage, either African American and Asian or African American and Indian, or some such origin. I was never able to track down any of his family to verify his ethnicity, and he wasn't telling. All the staff had their own guesses about "what Eldon is," but it really didn't matter. The only point that mattered, and the one that had one-hundred percent agreement, was that he was "Krazy" with a capital K.

I had really wanted to talk with Stiffeny and Nurse Kiki for a while, but Eldon's unwavering, dead-eyed, laser-like stare drew me away from the comfort of the nurse's station and out to the day room, where the patients were milling around waiting for morning medications. My GAS (give a shit) level to meet with him this early was pretty low, but I put on my best GAS smile and went over to Eldon. As I approached, he changed from a dead-eyed stare to a fuck-you stare. I don't think I can describe a fuck-you stare. It's like one senator said about pornography: "I can't tell you what it is but I know it when I see it." I was seeing the fuck-you stare. At this point, if I could have communicated with him by text, I would have done it. Talking with Eldon had lost its allure a long time before this impending meeting. He was "Karaizee" as hell and a whiner.

"What's up, Eldon?" I asked, hoping it was something as simple as him needing his attorney's phone number.

"I'm getting tired of it, and I want it to stop right now. I'm gonna blow up and tear this place apart if you don't make it stop. I want a grievance form to file on it."

I had seen him blow up before, and while he wasn't a karate master or anything like that, I didn't need this shit this early. And to top it off, him filling out a formal grievance form over what I suspected was some molecular-sized issue would wind up being a paperwork nightmare done just for paperwork's sake. Primarily it was an exercise in CYA (cover your ass). Very few patient grievances had any merit. Crazy, paranoid people think up crazy, paranoid shit. But, as per policy, we had to act like we were all very concerned and follow up all crazy, paranoid shit with an appropriate investigation.

"Hey, this seems important to you, so why don't you hold onto what's eating at you and let me get you in to see the treatment team first thing this morning," I said, trying to short circuit this before it got out of control. "That way you can tell everyone at once about this issue, and maybe we can resolve it without a formal grievance. Is that okay?"

"Yeah, I guess, but you better get me in."

Nurse Kiki got the charts ready for whenever Doctor Shrinkwrap would finally show up. The treatment team was supposed to meet at 9:00 a.m., Monday through Friday. Nurse Kiki and I were always ready and in our places at 9:00 sharp. Doctor Shrinkwrap was always late, every damn day. He would breeze into the treatment team room anywhere from fifteen to sixty minutes late. He always had some lame- ass excuse for being late, but the one today was the best in a long time.

"I was sitting out in my car waiting for Dr. Cork-screw and I fell asleep. When I woke up it was already 9:00, so I hurried to my office to get my stuff ready for today. You know Dr. Smellyme, the new guy from the Philippines who's only been here about a month — the one fresh out of school who has never had a real hospital job before but thinks he needs to tell everyone how this place should be run. He stopped me in the hall and started a bullshit brag session about how he wasn't using medication on his patients, but instead was using psychoanalytic psychoshit, and the training he was giving the staff on his unit, and how he is such a great and learned shrinkologist that incidents of violence on his unit have gone down by at least fifty percent since he got here, and now he is going to do the psychoanalytic psychoshit on the staff, and they are so thankful and appreciative that he is here. I happen to know for a fact that one of his patients hurt a staff member so bad that the staff member had to be sent to the emergency room. I also know for a fact that his staff thinks he is a Philippine shitbag. By the time he shut up, I had to go to the crapper. Did you know that there is only one-ply tissue in there? Anyway, while on the crapper I got a phone call, and when I looked at the time on my phone I realized that daylight saving time started last night, and so it was really 10 a.m. and not 9:00 a.m. when I woke up, so I got here as fast as I could. What's new with you guys?"

"What the hell, Doc. Do I need to babysit your ass every spring when the time changes, just so we can get some work done?" Nurse Kiki wasn't buying Doc's story. "We have about six patients to see this morning, but before we can get to any of them that screwed-up mess Eldon wants to see the treatment team. He has threatened to blow up if we don't see him first and take care of whatever has his panties in a knot."

"Couldn't you two handle it without me?" the doctor asked.

He always told us, "My job is to be here if you need me. Your job is to never need me." And he was serious. If anything ever came to his attention, then he would be forced to deal with it. He was a good doctor and could prescribe the right drugs in the right dose for the right patient with the right illness but, "you guys take care of all the other shit." Dealing with the other daily shit was not his forte.

"No can do today," I said. "Like Nurse Kiki said, this a full-blown treatment team issue. That is, unless you want to deal with it as a grievance."

"No, no, no, don't want that. Bring the crazy, little prick in here," he said.

I picked up the phone on the treatment team table, called Stiffeny, and asked her to send one of the PCAs with Eldon.

"Consider it done," she said.

A few minutes later, Eldon was seated across from the doctor. Nurse Kiki sat next to Eldon, and I was seated next to Dr. Shrinkwrap.

"John and Nurse Kiki tell me there is something wrong. Tell us about it."

"Well, Doc, it happens every night, and I want it to stop," he said angrily.

"What is it that happens? We need more information if we're going to make it better," Dr. Shrinkwrap said in his best GAS voice.

"They're having sex with me every night," Eldon choked out. "All night long they are having sex with me."

I sat up straight, because this kinda really did sound serious — a little, for a while. "Who is having sex with you?"

"Everybody is. The other patients, the guards, the staff, the people from town. They all line up down my hall and have their way with me. Sometimes it's in my ass; sometimes it's the other way. But it goes on all night, or until they have all had a turn."

Okay, not so serious now. This guy is not getting screwed all night long by every person within walking distance of his bed. However, I couldn't prove for a fact that it wasn't happening, so to continue seeming to GAS, I looked him in the eyes compassionately.

"That must make for a very long night for you," I said with a surprisingly straight face.

With an equally straight face, he looked me in the eye and said, "Naw, I sleep right through it."

Doc fell on the floor laughing, Nurse Kiki had to leave the room, and I was speechless.

A whole morning wasted.

Gilbert

The first time I met Gilbert was an exhausting and exhilarating ride of nonstop mental misconnections that manifested itself in an onslaught of verbal vomit. Gilbert was a good-looking black male in his mid-to-late twenties from a medium-sized city in our state. He was of average height but was of slight build. He had perfect skin, perfect straight white, evenly spaced teeth, and he spoke with perfect diction. He had been diagnosed early in his adult life as having bipolar disorder. The day I met him, he was at the peak of one of his manic phases.

It was early in the morning, before Dr. Shrinkwrap had arrived on the unit. Gilbert had been admitted late on the previous day, and I had not had a chance to meet him. I was at the nurse's station looking at his chart and chatting up Nurse Kiki and Stiffeny.

"What do you know about this new guy?" I asked between flirtations with them.

"Well, I think he's probably a pretty good kid, but he is sick as hell right now. I just met him this morning myself, and it was quite the psychotic train wreck," Nurse Kiki said with a grin.

"Yeah, I think you should meet him this morning and get the full "Gilbert experience" before Doc gets ahold of him and messes things up," Stiffeny said with a conspiratorial grin.

"How could Doc mess things up?"

"I just don't think Gilbert will be Gilbert with a couple of weeks of psychotropic medicine down his throat. Today is the optimal Gilbert day. Go get 'em, tiger."

"Okay, have one of the PCAs bring him back to the treatment room, and I'll meet him and talk to him."

"I'll have one do that, but I think you'll wind up doing more meeting him than talking to him."

"Whatever."

I didn't have to wait too long for my "Gilbert experience" to begin. I had just settled into the treatment room to await the delivery of our new patient when I heard some high-volume verbiage headed down the hall in my direction. The door swung open and the PCA unloaded Gilbert with a kind of haste that made me think a) Gilbert needs a bath, b) Gilbert has lice, or c) a combination of both. It was neither. My hint should have been when the PCA looked at me, put his hands over his ears, shook his head, rolled his eyes, and mouthed "Good luck."

Gilbert sat down in front of me.

"So you're Mr. John Booth," he began without an introduction. "Is that like a telephone booth or a toll booth it doesn't matter cause you know they don't have telephone booths anymore and I don't drive so a toll booth is just stupid but it could be like a booth at a restaurant cause I 've been to a restaurant once or was it a café hey your name sounds like the guy that shot Lincoln right square in the head but it's probably not you cause you're too young and a little too white but I bet you know the guy or are related to the guy who shot Lincoln I found a Lincoln head penny once I bet you had one too it was real pretty and shiny but it got unpretty the longer I had it do you have a Lincoln car my uncle had a Lincoln car and it was shiny like my penny but he broke it somehow and now has a Chrysler that he let me take to the drive- in movie but I didn't have a date or anything but I bet you have been to a lot of drive-in movies have you ever been to a drive-in movie I bet you've been to a lot of drive-in movies I bet you took girls to the drive-in movies and had sex in the backseat or the front seat if it laid down but I bet that would be cold with your skinny white ass sticking up in the air without any covers or anything but back to me it was real nice and cool the night I went to the drive-in movie not at all like last night when it was so hot boy was it hot last night and I didn't think I was ever going to get to sleep even if I could've had sex which I didn't even though I slept naked like back at jail where I slept naked too and I didn't have any sex there either except this one older guy had sex with me but I didn't have sex back with him even after he said I could and I was naked and all cause it was hot but it was a little scary I mean not him but the bugs but mostly I was scared of the spiders I think they was spiders they felt like spiders I didn't like it when they crawled on my private parts cause you know they're private and if a spider bites your private parts it can be real bad and it can swell up not in a good way and it hurts real bad and I heard of a guy who had his private part bit one time by a spider and it swelled up not in the good way and it started to turn all black and blue and die and I was told that they had to cut his private part off before it fell off so spiders are off limits but I had an ant farm once when I was little it's funny cause my ant farm was given to me by my uncle get it I had an ant farm

but we didn't live on a farm that had ants farms have
cows and horses and chickens that lay eggs that are
pretty cool cause you can do a lot of things with eggs
scramble them fry them hard boil them make egg
salad color them for Easter throw them at houses at
Halloween or at a girl when she makes fun of you
at school when you dribble pee pee and your pants
get wet in front and I know I've said this before but
I bet you've been with a lot of girls I mean had sex
with them and touched each other's private parts like
touched her private parts with your private parts I
don't think I've had sex with a girl yet but maybe I
grew up in a house in a city and didn't go to private
school I thought of that cause I said private parts a
lot a minute ago some kids went to private school
and some went to public school I just went to public
school cause we weren't rich like the private school
families that had kids who wore uniforms to private
school and it looked like they wore the same thing
every day but I wore the same thing every day and
nobody called it a uniform I wonder if private school
kids grew up to be private investigators they call them
PIs in all the TV shows when I was a kid I thought I
wanted to be a private investigator but they have to
sit for a really really long long time in cars and look
and people go by and I couldn't sit for a really really
long long time in a car without peeing on myself then
the girls would make fun of me again so PI is out but
I had a black eye once and the pink eye a couple of
times I had my eyes checked and the doctor said I got
twenty twenty vision twenty twenty would be even
odds at a race track like that one in the picture over
there on the wall I bet the horse's name is Seabiscuit
what is a Seabiscuit any way I ran track for a while

in school cause it would get you out of some other classes it was okay except all the boys were in the locker room together and all our private parts were hanging out all at once and everybody could see who had the longest and who had the shortest and the fattest but mine wasn't the shortest or the skinniest and no one laughed at me like we did at the guys with the little skinny ones in the lower classes we were in the lower class but my folks called up middle class but the other folks who said they were middle class seemed to be a long ways off from us the folks on Happy Days were middle class he owned a hardware store or something why do they call it a hardware store almost like hard-on when I get a hard-on I jerk off some guys call it beat off but I jack off and sex is fun but I don't do it accept by myself all the time mostly jack off I had Jack Daniel whiskey once and got real drunk and threw up and I didn't feel good the next morning and I was real thirsty and drank a lot of water but camels don't need a lot of water cause they carry it with them in their hump on their back I think hump on their back sounds like sex but it's not and camels aren't at all like cows with three stomachs that chew their cud that sounds a little like cuddle but I know it's not the same cuddle then there's candle like burn the candle at both ends which sounds crazy to me cause your candle would burn up too fast like my momma's house did when I set it on fire and they arrested me when I was trying to do a good thing for my mamma who worked so hard and deserved a new house from the insurance money so I burned the old one down I guess I should have told mamma to get out of the house first but ain't life funny that way how you forget to do something that later seems like it would have been important I don' t think I've had much or any sex yet so I think when I go to trial I will just plead guilty and go to prison and turn gay."

"Alrighty then."

A Little More About Gilbert

The treatment team was between seeing patients and engaged in our two favorite pastimes: bad mouthing the administrator of the hospital and/or making fun of our patients. Dr. Shrinkwrap had the floor and was ranting in detail and at length about his latest meeting with the superintendent of the hospital. "And I told that little motherfucker that it was an insult to my standing as a physician and that they had better not ever again put goddamn one-ply tissue in the shitter outside my office."

I had heard this and many other rants before. Luckily Stiffany riotously burst into the room and breathlessly announced, "Gilbert is going sideways crazy."

"What the hell does 'sideways crazy' mean?" asked Doctor Shrinkwrap, always the stickler for detail.

"What I mean," Stiffany said with a definite edge, "is that the little asshole refused to take his medication. He told the med nurse that you had changed his pills without telling him, and he wasn't taking any of that poison, and she could shove it up her ass. The med nurse tried to sweet talk him into it, but he would have none of it. Finally the med nurse told him that if he didn't take the pills she would be forced to give him the medication in an injection. Then the shit really hit the fan."

Doctor Shrinkwrap grabbed Gilbert's chart and began looking at the legal papers at the back.

"We have an order to treat the little fart, don't we? Yeah, here it is. Tell Gilbert that he needs to get it into his psychotic shit cup that he calls a head that he does not have the right to refuse medication and that we most assuredly will pump his ass full of medication if he does not willingly take his pills. But say it in a nice way, will yah, hon?"

Stiffany left the room and came back shortly.

"Well, I tried, but the little shit got even madder and ran to his room and climbed on top of the bookcase. He won't come down now, no matter how much I lie to him about what is going to happen."

Nurse Kiki sighed, got up, and started for the door, but stopped and sat back down.

"Call security and let them fuck with him."

Stiffany rolled her eyes.

"I already gave the Gestapo a call, but he insists on talking to one of you guys."

I looked at Dr. Shrinkwrap, who immediately grabbed and opened another patient's chart. This was his nonverbal signal that he was not going to deal with this shit.

"Why does he want to talk to one of us?" I asked.

Stiffany shrugged.

"How the hell should I know. He's fucking crazier that a pet coon. You guys are the 'experts'. Come in here, talk to the little shithead, and get him the hell off that bookcase so I can get my work done. I don't have time and I don't get paid enough to fuck with his crazy crap."

Doc. Shrinkwrap looked at me.

"John, why don't you go handle it while Nurse

Kiki and I discuss treatment options."

I knew that was coming. It always lands on the social worker to deal with this type of crap. I got up, left the treatment room, went down the hall to the unit, used my cardkey to unlock the unit, and went in. I crossed the dayroom where the other patients were watching TV and playing cards and went down the hall on the left. Gilbert's room was about halfway down the hall. The door was open, and a couple of PCAs were standing just outside his room trying to coax Gilbert down. They saw me coming, stepped back out of the way, and gave me a "tag, you're it" gesture.

I went into the room and sure enough, there was Gilbert about seven feet off the ground, on the top of his bookcase. He had the scared, crazy eyes I had seen a thousand times before from patients who felt trapped. I wanted to tread lightly, so I stopped just inside the doorway.

"Hey, buddy, what the fuck are you doing?" I asked softly.

He looked at me and screamed, "They want to put a needle in my ass."

"Nobody wants to stick a needle in your ass," I said softly after taking another half step into the room. "Just take the pills, and your ass will stay unstuck."

If it was possible, his voice rose another octave.

"Are you too stupid to get it?" he yelled. "I ain't takin' no fucking psycho pills, and you ain't gonna give me no psycho med shot in my ass. And I ain't comin' down. So, fuck you."

Negotiations continued in this vein for a few more minutes with no real anticipation of resolutions, but rather, to document on the ever-present video recording that a win/win conclusion had been attempted. Experience had proven that we were way past anything close to a win/win outcome. Gilbert was way too crazy, and the situation had escalated way too far. He wasn't going to play nice.

In collaboration with Stiffany and the PCAs, it was determined that, for his safety and ours, he needed to be forcibly brought down from the bookcase. Stiffany went to the nurse's station by the dayroom and called hospital security. About five minutes later, Officer Headlock and five other security officers came crashing into the dayroom like fucking John Wayne storming Normandy Beach on D-Day.

Stiffany put up her hands to slow them down, and then motioned them to the nurses station. I heard their entrance and moved from Gilbert's room to the nurses station. Stiffany and I apprised Officer Headlock of the situation. He gathered his troops in a corner of the dayroom, where they huddled and devised a plan of action.

When the huddle broke, he came over to Stiffany and me.

"Here's what we're gonna do," he said. "First we are gonna spread mattresses on the floor of his room so no one gets hurt when — I mean if — he gets knocked off the bookcase. Next, we will rush in there like the fucking light brigade and yank his skinny ass off there before he can take a breath and ask God for help. Then we will hold the little fucker down so the med nurse can give him a shot in his skinny ass."

Stiffany and I agreed that it was as good a plan as any, so we gave the thumbs-up and the plan was set in motion. Mattresses were taken from six other rooms and were spread out on the floor below Gilbert.

Security lined up outside his room in preparation to rush in, secure him, and save the day. Officer Headlock gave the "go ahead" nod to the troops, but before they could make their move, Gilbert seemed to wake up to the impending battle.

"I'm going to fucking Superman kick all your fucking asses," he screamed.

He let out a heart-stopping scream/war cry and leaped from the top of the bookcase — at which point everything went wrong.

His leap was miscalculated. He jumped too hard and hit the top of his head on the ceiling. This impact caused him to do a quarter turn in midair, altering his trajectory and allowing his forehead to slam into the concrete wall to his left. This in turn caused him to fall to the cement floor, missing the "safety mattresses" by about two feet. We all just stood there in amazement, as he lay there unceremoniously unconscious. He had a lump as big as my fist on the top of his head and a gash about three inches long that creased his forehead, giving him what appeared to be a bright red third eyebrow. The poor bastard was bleeding like a stuck pig. The med nurse rushed in, popped a needle in his ass, and pumped in a liberal dose of Haldol and Benadryl. Gilbert was loaded on a gurney to be taken to the med clinic to be stitched up.

Officer Headlock and the five officers gave high fives all around for a job well done, and I went back to the treatment room. Upon my entry, Doctor Shrinkwrap and Nurse Kiki jumped apart, grabbed two charts and gave me the "nothing to see here" look.

Back to business as usual.

Jerry

I met Jerry early on in my social work career, way back when there was still a state-run mental health hospital. He was a tall, muscular, good-looking black man who always had a smile on his face and a red baseball cap on his head. He never met a stranger, and honestly, no one ever met anyone stranger than Jerry.

He had been diagnosed with mental illness since his late teens. I got to know him in his middle twenties, and watched as he became a "revolving door" or "frequent flyer" patient. He was from a town in our state that was small enough that everybody knew everybody else and everybody knew Jerry. Whether crazy or well, Jerry had the ability to "shoot the shit" with anyone on just about any topic. He was just as good at listening as he was at talking and made a great "buddy" to team up with new patients who were admitted to the hospital. He knew his way around the hospital and grounds, was kind and empathetic, and would suffer through hours of incoherent babbling from new patients without a complaint.

With Jerry, the "revolving door" pattern started immediately after his first admission and subsequent discharge from the hospital. We sent him home with two weeks of medication, an outpatient appointment to his community mental health center, and the anticipation that we would never see him again. Jerry, however, either did not or would not recognize that he had a mental illness and resented the fact that the "Goddamn doctor keeps insisting that I take these goddam mental pills."

He would take the "mental pills" as long as the first prescription lasted, and not a day or a pill more. When Jerry was not taking his "mental pills," he was one of the sickest patients I have ever worked with. The auditory hallucinations (voices no one else hears) and visual hallucinations (seeing things no one else sees) would alternately torment him and entertain him, and whether being tormented or entertained by his hallucinations, they were his reality. With such a screwed-up version of reality, his brain was constantly being fed bad information. With bad information going into his brain, bad decisions would come out of his brain. Bad decisions would lead to bad actions that would lead to attentions from the community, and not in a good way. When he would draw the bad attention, in a very short time, he would be sent back to the hospital.

As I said before, everybody in Jerry's town knew Jerry. Over the years, they began to understand that he was crazy as hell and gradually started to tolerate his psychosis-induced, erratic behavior more and more. Inevitably, however, he would do something really outrageous, or as Jerry put it, "I would pull a dumb ass." That was when the police would be called and he would wind up back at the hospital. This routine went on for years. Then...

It had been about nine months since Jerry had been discharged from the hospital, and no one had heard a word from him or about him. We were convinced that our years of passionate, persistent, and concentrated effort (read: years of nagging his ass) had finally paid dividends. We had worked magic, and Jerry was insightful and understood the benefits of seeing his doctor and taking his medication. He would at long last lead a productive life, and it was our good works that had made it happen.

We were so full of shit. It wasn't long after we began patting ourselves on the back that Jerry screwed up. But he didn't screw up just a little this time. This time it was huge. This one bat-shit-crazy, over-the-top, hallucination-laden, irrational act elevated him to legendary status and made him the most memorable patient we would ever have. He told me later, "Hallucination-wise, this motherfucker was an ass kicker!" I couldn't have agreed more.

As I said, he had been away from the hospital and back in his hometown for about nine months. During that time he had not taken one milligram of "crazy pills," and his symptoms of mental illness were really starting to kick his ass now. He was responding to hallucinations and talking to people who weren't there most of every day. On his last day of freedom, Jerry went to the downtown business district of his community. As was his usual custom, he began wandering the streets. His wanderings lead him past one of the largest Baptist churches in the area, The First Holiness Hold My Mule Shout To The Lord And Praise His Name Gospel Tabernacle Tower Of Power Healing And Virginity Restoration Church And Youth Basketball Center Inc., Rev. Thelodious Hankey, Minister.

We don't know, because Jerry never really said, why he made a right hand turn and went into the church. Maybe it was the music that drew him in, or maybe one of his voices told him to go in. Either way, Jerry entered the church just in time for the funeral of Cornelia Mae (Grandma) Tucker. Dressed in dirty blue jeans, torn and soiled white tee shirt, day glow orange flip flops, and a red baseball cap, Jerry strode through the lobby, down the center aisle of the church, and didn't break stride until he was front and center, staring at the poor, old, shroud-draped dead body of Cornelia Mae (Grandma) Tucker lying in her mahogany casket. Jerry then doubled up his fist, banged on the coffin lid as hard as he could, grabbed Cornelia Mae (Grandma) Tucker by the shoulders, gave her a good shake, and in a thunderous voice that still echoes in the ears of the mourners, yelled, "WAKE UP, BITCH AND FIX ME SOME CHICKEN."

After Cornelia Mae (Grandma) Tucker's grandsons got through kicking the living shit out of Jerry, they debated on whether to call the police or kick the shit out of him some more. The Rev. Thelodious Hankey intervened on Jerry's behalf and convinced the family of Cornelia Mae (Grandma) Tucker that the Lord preached that all things should be in moderation and it wouldn't be Christian to kick the shit out of Jerry any more. It was reluctantly agreed all around that kicking the shit out of Jerry some more might accidentally be a sin, especially if done in The First Holiness Hold My Mule Shout To The Lord And Praise His Name Gospel Tabernacle Tower Of Power Healing And Virginity Restoration And Youth Basketball Center Inc., and it was probably best to be Christian and follow the prudent course of action to call the police and let them kick the shit out of him for them.

The police were called. The first time Jerry opened his mouth, they obliged the family and proceeded to kick the living shit out of him. Once Jerry shut up, he was locked up and summarily returned to the hospital. BudiBudiBudi....That's all folks!

Sergio

Sergio was one of our forensic patients who had been accused of a crime but could not go to trial because he had been found to be incompetent to stand trial due to mental illness. The crime he was accused of was Indecent Exposure to a Minor Child Under The Age of Sixteen. He was court ordered to our hospital to undergo competency restoration treatment.

Sergio was one generation removed from a family of illegal Mexicans who came to the Estados Unidos to better their lives by taking jobs from U.S. citizens, abusing the welfare system, overrunning the schools, not learning English, being offended every Cinco De Mayo when someone wears an American flag tee shirt, and feeling ever so entitled to do so. He was of average to slight build, about 5'9" tall, and had short-cropped black hair and a thick accent that gave away the fact that English was not spoken in his home. He was wearing his orange jailhouse jumpsuit when Doctor Shrinkwrap and I met him in the admissions area of the hospital. We peeked in the small, wire-reinforced glass window of the solid metal door that was the entry to the room where he was being held. He was a little uneasy, marked by constant fidgeting and squirming in his chair, until we walked in the room. At that point, he straightened up in his chair and a fuck-you countenance spread across his face.

We entered the room, and Dr. Shrinkwrap and I took places behind the desk and motioned for Sergio to take a seat across from us. Nurse Kiki came into the room, rolling a desk chair with her. She took her usual place next to Dr. Shrinkwrap.

Dr. Shrinkwrap always preached to the treatment team that he had been taught that it was vital to establish a rapport with the patient as quickly as possible by finding some common ground. On this occasion, Doctor Shrinkwrap chose to use Pig Spanish as his rapport-building tool. He reached across the desk, thrusting his hand out to Sergio, and said, "Put her there, muchachio. What brings you to our haciender? Do you speako any Englisho?"

Nurse Kiki jumped into the breach and asked, "Do you speak any English?"

"Si, I speak English, some, a little bit good."

Wanting to establish the charade that I give a shit, I also thrust out my hand. "Hey, where you from? You been around here long, buddy?"

Looking me dead in the eyes he said softly, "I was born in the Estado Unidos."

Holy shit, this guy has been in the United States his whole life and only speaks English "a little bit good" and can't call the United States the United States but instead, calls the United States of America the Estado Unidos. Fuck him.

Looking confused, Nurse Kiki explains to Doctor Shrinkwrap that Estado Unidos means the United States. "Do you know where you are right now, muchachio?" he asks. "Do you know what this place is?"

"No."

"Would you like to know where you are?" I inquire,

attempting to continue my disguise as someone who gives a shit.

Sergio nods his head.

"Well, my brother from another mother," I begin "you are in a mental health hospital, the nut house, the crazy farm. You've been accused of a crime but can't go to trial because the judge thought you were incompetent to stand trial due to mental illness. Do you understand what I mean?"

Sergio gives me a blank stare. I give him one back, hoping that with silence and time what I said will sink in and he will understand. Wrong.

I try again, using the Doctor Shrinkwrap approach.

"Let me put it this way. You are in the nutto houso. Comprendo?"

Blank stare from Sergio.

Undaunted, I soldier on in English.

"You were picked up by the police and arrested. The judge says you broke the law, and you now have a criminal charge."

He gives a small nod, indicating a modicum of understanding. Now we're getting somewhere.

"Can you tell me what happened?"

"I pulled my dick out on a girl," Sergio says, then averts his eyes from Nurse Kiki.

The first part of being found competent is to know what you are charged with, so I ask him, "Yeah, that's what they say you did all right, but do you know what your charge is?"

Sergio reverted to the blank stare for a while, then shrugged his shoulders and scrunched up his face in the universal sign indicating, "I don't know what the fuck you mean."

"I pulled my dick out on a girl," he restated.

"Okay, you pulled your dick out on a girl. I get it. That was the behavior that got you arrested, but what is your charge?"

Sergio continued in his befuddlement, and like a myna bird said, "I pulled my dick out on a girl."

I'm getting a little tired of this shit, but determined to make a point, I try one more time.

"You pulled your dick out on a girl. What is the charge for doing that?"

At that point a light bulb goes on in Sergio's head, and he gets a self-assured look on his face like he knows he finally knows the right answer. He sits up straight in his chair, pulls his shoulders back, puffs up his chest, and proudly states, "I pulled my dick out on a girl, but there is no charge. I did it for free."

Nurse Kiki falls on the floor laughing. Doctor Shrinkwrap sneaks a peek up her skirt. I run out of the room to tell the rest of the staff before I forget what this dumb fuck said.

After working with Sergio daily for two years, the psychology department determined that he would never be able to attain competency. He was sent to court and ordered to be transferred to another state mental hospital. He was held there for two weeks and was deemed to not be a danger to himself or others and was released back into the world.

God bless America.

Poor Pitiful Paul

Paul, Paul, Poor Pitiful Paul. If you have ever seen the Christmas story about "Rudolph the Red-Nosed Reindeer," then you are familiar with the Island of Misfit Toys. Poor Pitiful Paul could have been the poster child for the Island of Misfit Toys. Not only was Poor Pitiful Paul profoundly mentally ill, but he was also one of the ugliest human beings that I or anyone else had or ever will lay eyes on.

I mean, this guy was more than just semi-ugly — he was the total package ugly. To start off, his posture was slouched to the point of resembling Quasimodo and was exacerbated by a shuffling gait that kicked up a cloud of dust that would have rivaled the Peanuts character, Pig Pen. His head is lopsided and conical, resembling a newborn baby's head that never achieved normal shape.

On the front of his head is a face that is divided by a nose that has seen too many fists. This battered portal makes an almost ninety-degree right-hand turn that gives it the appearance of being not quite centered. It is impossible to determine how long this schnozzola should have been, because a rat or rats had chewed off a portion of the tip when he was an infant. The story is that he had been placed in foster care nearly immediately after birth due to being born to hopelessly drug-addicted parents. Whoever his "caregiver" was lived in a filthy shithole of a shack on the outskirts of town.

As the story goes, it was the caregiver's custom to bathe Poor Pitiful Paul weekly, whether he needed it or not. If you have ever had a kid, you know that even one day of poop, piss, and baby food is too much to imagine being left on a child. It's hard to conjure up how disgusting he must have been with seven days of encrusted baby food on his face and feces on his ass. Nothing is too disgusting for rats. The rats didn't call it disgusting — they called it dinner. So, one night, in an overzealous eating frenzy of caked-on split peas, creamed corn, cream of wheat, pureed carrots, and Similac, the rat/rats digested a portion of his nose along with the aforementioned caked-on food. But I digress. To make the nose worse, if that is possible, it was tinged a greyish-blue color that was caused by either large doses of Thorazine over a long period of time, emphysema, or both.

He has a perpetual case of acne that causes dime-sized purple pustules to erupt across his face, nose, forehead, neck, back, and shoulders. The few teeth he had left — think Jack-o'-lantern — were flecked with a greenish mold that seemed to be embedded in the enamel itself. And if life hadn't crapped on this guy enough, he was inflicted with a condition that created chronic body odor that enshrouded his body from a yet-to-be-identified body part. The aides made a point of bathing him daily but to no avail.

Nurse Kiki and I are convinced that prolonged exposure to this funk by anyone other than Poor Pitiful Paul would be life threatening and /or cause abnormalities in offspring of those in its proximity. But, despite having the mother lode of repulsivity, Poor

Pitiful Paul had the one thing we all want and live for: He had someone to love. Poor Pitiful Paul had Lerlene. He believed her to not only be his girlfriend but also his soul mate, light of his life, his reason to live, and the potential mother of his children. (God help us.) Aah, but fate is an evil bitch.

Surprise, surprise. Poor Pitiful Paul suffered from depression. On top of that, he had a mixed bag of psychotic features, which means that along with his depression, he heard and saw shit nobody else heard or saw. In technical terms, he hallucinated his ass off. Poor Pitiful Paul once told me he couldn't remember not being fucked up mentally. Then he met Lerlene, a tomboyish girl who wore nothing but blue jeans and stained tee shirts and was only slightly less ugly than Poor Pitiful Paul. She cussed like a sailor, but in a disarmingly charming Southern drawl. Lerlene was a very outgoing soul who never met a stranger, and she was nuttier that squirrel shit.

Poor Pitiful Paul and Lerlene lived on different wards at the hospital, but their paths serendipitously crossed one day while out on the hospital grounds. They were both headed to the canteen for a smoke and a coke. Poor Pitiful Paul was drawn to Lerlene from the time he first laid eyes on her. He thought she was everything he ever wanted or hoped for. They had "dated" for about three weeks. By dated, I mean they held hands while walking to the canteen, watched movies together at the Patients Activity Center, and danced together at socials arranged by the recreation department of the hospital. They had been together long enough for Poor Pitiful Paul to believe he had found Miss Right, and he was in love.

Since the introduction of Lerlene into his life, his

depression had been on the backburner. He had been going around with a spring in his step, a gleam in his eye, a song in his heart, and an erection in his pants. It was his day to be seen by the treatment team, and as soon as Stiffany brought him into the treatment room, it was obvious that the old Poor Pitiful Paul had returned. His posture was more slouched, his movements were lethargic, he hadn't shaved, his hair stuck out in a thousand little different directions, and he had no observable hard-on. His eyes were downcast, and the rivulets created by tears gave away the fact that he had been crying.

Doctor Shrinkwrap looked at me and mouthed, "Oh shit, what now?"

Nurse Kiki kicked Doctor Shrinkwrap under the table and gave him her "knock it the fuck off and get serious" look. Being the professional that he is, the doctor seamlessly transitioned to his psychiatrist face and focused back on Poor Pitiful Paul.

He sincerely looked at Poor Pitiful Paul, and with his practiced and professional shrinkologist voice asked, "Hey, what's the matter? You look like hammered shit, pal."

Nurse Kiki, sensing a need to jump in, put on her GAS face and said, "What Doctor Shrinkwrap means is that you don't look like yourself today, and he is concerned. Your state of mind and your well-being are at the forefront of his attention. Right, Doc?"

Doctor Shrinkwrap looked up, and with an almost imperceptible eye roll, muttered, "Yeah, your state of mind, best interest, and what not."

Without prompting, Poor Pitiful Paul began in a soft monotone, "You fuckers think I look like hammered shit. Well, you fuckers wouldn't look so hot yourselves if your life sucked like mine does and you had been mind fucked like I've been mind fucked."

Doctor Shrinkwrap, feigning some degree of GAS, picked up the Diagnostic and Statistics Manual and whispered to himself as he thumbed through it, "Mind fucked, mind fucked. What does that mean, mind fucked?"

"What it means, dumb fuck," Poor Pitiful Paul growled, "is that mother fucker bitch has been fucking with me and fucking up my mind. Get it? Mind fucked, you motherfucker."

What little vocabulary Poor Pitiful Paul had diminished measurably with his increased anger and psychosis. When he would get to this point, his primary adjectives and adverbs were fucker, fucking, fucking fucker, motherfucker, fucking fuckerhead, mother fucking fuckerhead, and various combinations of these.

Using my Spider-Man like senses, and my impeccable clinical judgment and expertice, I determined that Poor Pitiful Paul was, as he put it, "one fucking pissed off fucking mother fucking fuckerhead" and elected to keep my mouth shut the fuck up and stay the hell out of this discussion.

Doctor Shrinkwrap looked up from the Diagnostic and Statistics Manual.

"I think I have found your new diagnosis in here," he said with a straight face. "The technical psychological diagnosis for what you have is Holyfuckmeosis. But I could be wrong. What the hell happened to get you like this?"

"It's Lerlene, my girlfriend," Poor Pitiful Paul began, with his eyes staring a hole in the floor.

Doctor Shrinkwrap gingerly moved forward,

placed his hand under Poor Pitiful Paul's chin, and lifted his face up so he could look him in the eye.

"Oh yeah, women, can't live with them and can't live without them," he said to Poor Pitiful Paul with a guys' club wink. "Am I right?"

With that, Nurse Kiki reached under the table, grabbed Doctor Shrinkwrap by the balls, and fixed him with a cold stare that silently told him, "I know something you'll be living without if you don't straighten the fuck up."

Being the learned man that he is, Doctor Shrinkwrap got the message loud and clear. He looked over at Poor Pitiful Paul, and affecting his shrinkologist voice again, he said, "Okay, fella, talk to me about your girlfriend, Lerlene."

You could tell that Poor Pitiful Paul was uncomfortable with the thought of talking about it. He squirmed in his chair, rubbed his forehead with his right hand, and balled up a used tissue with his left hand. After a moment of summoning up his courage, he cleared his throat, and in as sad a voice as I have ever heard, he began.

"Lerlene is supposed to be my girlfriend, but she's been going around the grounds, sneaking behind bushes, and trading cigarettes for sex with other guys. Doc, you know, I don't think it's right for her to do that, you know, trading sex for cigarettes with other guys when she's supposed to be my girl. It can't be right, I tell ya. Sex for cigarettes, all day long, when I'm not around. Sex for cigarettes when she's supposed to be my girl. It ain't right, it ain't right. Sex for cigarettes, sex for cigarettes all day long, sex for cigarettes."

Seemingly exhausted, Poor Pitiful Paul took a deep

breath, sighed, shook his head, and softly and sadly said, "She sure does smoke a lot."

Footnote: a few years later, Lerlene died of lung cancer.

Pam W.

Pam W. was one of the first patients I met at the old mental health hospital. I remember her because the first thing she ever said to me was, "I'm going to kill myself someday." I was shocked that someone would be so blunt about suicide.

"No, you're not," I told her. "You are in a super safe place, and we are never going to let that happen." She made a liar out of me.

Pam W. was a tall, not skinny but not fat girl who by all accounts had "not been right" for most of her life. Her official education had been minimal, mostly in special education classes and short term. For the four years that I knew her, she had no identifiable support system other than the hospital. No friends other than her fellow patients and the hospital staff. No birthday cards. No Christmas cards. She never had a visitor or a phone call. She did have a family — mother, father and a couple of sisters — but it seemed to them that Pam was best "out of sight, out of mind."

She could piss you off and make you love her all in the same day. She knew she was crazy and depressed, and wrapped herself in insanity's embrace and made it her identity. She had been in so many inpatient settings and so many therapies that she could almost direct a group therapy session by herself. She, sometimes, made admirably insightful comments to other patients.

She, sometimes, made incredibly cruel comments to other patients.

She was probably a lesbian. She had a right cross that felt like a mule had kicked you, followed by the sincere remorse of a child. She could, would, and did swallow almost anything. I have seen x-rays showing paraphernalia she had swallowed. Pens, pencils, paper clips, plastic spoons, plastic forks, crayons, chalk, staples, small balls, handfuls of tacks, etc. If it could fit in her mouth, she would chuck it down her throat and dare you to try and stop her. I always thought she could have made a fortune working that act in a carnival midway freak show. Maybe in a future life.

Pam's physical appearance screamed, "I'M CRAZY!!!!" She wore nothing but state hospital issued clothes. If you have ever seen state mental hospital issued clothes, you know they are less than flattering for man or woman. They are plain; straight lined; utilitarian; either tan, gray, or blue in color; and look like they came from the ready-to-wear rack in a politburo-owned store in Russia. For Pam, it looked like they had been designed with her in mind. Looking back, I can't imagine her in anything else. Pleated dresses, starched blouses, and polished shoes would have looked as out of place on her as a tuxedo on a monkey.

Pam wore her hair in a very short, cropped cut that looked self-inflicted. Speaking of self-infliction, the most noticeable element of Pam's physical appearance were the scars up and down each arm. Permanent reminders from God of each time she had tried to kill herself/demand attention. Remarkably, she had each one mentally cataloged. If asked, she could point to any of the scars and give its history. How long ago

54

she had made the cut, what she had used to cut herself with, how many stitches it took to close the wound, how much it hurt on a one-to-ten scale, and how long it took to heal. She could also tell you which ones were legitimate suicide attempts and which were not.

At times I was sure that Pam was proud of her never-ending self-mutilation. If there had ever been an extended length of time since her last flesh-gashing stroke from a piece of glass or purloined razor blade, the staff would take notice. With implicit understanding, they would begin to watch her more closely, with the historical knowledge that another battle in the war of Pam W. verses Pam W. was in the near future.

I don't mean to paint a picture of a girl who was chronically in a state of suicidal depression. Quite the contrary. Pam was quick to laugh and quick to joke. She attended all dances, parties, picnics, and outings off the unit, and took and active role in all. But for me, at least, the most mystifying characteristic Pam had was the capacity to do self-harm while seeming to be having fun. On more than one occasion, she would be in attendance of or have just left a party, picnic, dance, etc., and still make a savage cut to her arm. And Pam never just scratched herself. She cut with purpose and passion.

As I may have said before, each day at the hospital was pretty much like every other day. Each unit and each person on each unit had their own routine, rhythm, and role. Some joked all day, and some worked all day. Some were easily engaged in conversation, and some always kept to themselves. Some always smoked, and some always bitched about those smoking. You get the picture — a yin for every yang. Because of the fixed routine and regularity of the roles, any alteration was conspicuous.

My routine was to enter the unit early, and with a smile. I would seek out the head nurse, who at that time of day was always behind the nurse's station, and ask, "Who are we going to fix today?"

"We don't fix anybody," would invariably be her response. "We just continually work on them."

The patients were always milling around, preparing to go to breakfast. The TV was always tuned to the "Today Show." The nurse would inform me of any new admission from the night before. She and I would go over the list of patients to be seen by the treatment team, grab their respective charts from the chart rack, and take them to the treatment room. Each unit had a break room furnished with a coffee pot, microwave oven, small table and chairs, small refrigerator, sink, coffee, cups, a clock, and usually a cake or brownies brought from someone's home kitchen. I would take a cup of coffee from the break room back to the treatment room and chat with anyone who wandered by while I was waiting for the doctor to show up.

I don't remember the date or the day of the week it happened, but just like I remember the first day I met Pam W., I remember the morning the routine and rhythm were thrown into disorder.

On that morning I parked my old, green Ford LTD in the parking lot across from the entrance to the building that housed my patients, crossed the street, and bounded up the concrete steps. I turned right and swung by my office to pick up my notebook, then went to the second floor, taking the stairs instead of the ancient elevator. I pulled out my key and unlocked the main door to the unit. I walked down a wood-floored corridor that was flanked on each side by bunk beds and lockers used by the patients. It looked like a ghost town. Not a soul in that area.

I walked on down to the day room, a large open space with the nurse's station on one end, metal-barred windows on two sides, glaring florescent lights overhead, and a television on the remaining wall. The television was turned off, and the patients were sitting quietly in the metal-framed chairs that ringed the room. The aids were standing in twos and threes talking quietly. They acknowledged my entrance with a silent nod.

I got an uh-oh sensation in my gut and proceeded to the nurse's station. No nurse. I checked the treatment room. Empty. More uh-oh. I turned and came back up the hall to the break room. The nurse was there, sitting on a rusted metal chair on the far side of the wooden table with a half-drunk cup of black coffee in her hand. When she looked up, the sensation I had before took a dramatic upgrade from "uh-oh" to "what the hell." The nurse looked just like you would imagine a person to look when they have been told that the unthinkable had just become reality. I walked over to her side of the table and put my hand on her shoulder.

"What's going on around here?" I asked. "It's so quiet. Whatever it is, it can't be good. You look like you just lost your best friend."

"Pam W. is dead," she whispered.

I gave her shoulder a squeeze, got a cup of coffee, and pulled one of the mismatched metal chairs across the table from her.

"What did she do?" I asked, expecting to hear that Pam W. had finally arranged to cut herself deeply enough and far enough away from help that she bled to death.

The nurse sat up straight, figuratively put on her professional nurses cap, and explained the circumstances of the death of Pam W.

"She hung herself in the bathroom. One of the overnight PCAs found her when they were making their half-hour rounds. It appears she got out of bed and took a bed sheet with her without anyone seeing her. She tied one end around the frame of one of the toilet stalls and the other end around her neck. It looks like she then just fell forward, with her neck taking the impact of her body weight. She didn't strangle. Her neck was broken."

"She really did it," I said to no one in particular.

"Yeah, her body is already at the funeral home in town," she replied.

The census of the hospital, and similarly the unit I was working, had inflated to the point that more than one social worker was required to adequately cover the patient load. Because of this, Pam W. was not part of my caseload any longer. I went to Pam's social worker's office to offer any assistance I could give in making arrangements, contacting family, etc.

"No, the family has been contacted, and they are taking care of all of the funeral arrangements. They have decided to have her buried in the hospital cemetery, but I don't know when yet. I will let you know when I know," she said.

Two days later, a graveside funeral service was held at the hospital cemetery located about a mile from the main cluster of buildings. After having dug the grave with one of the hospital backhoes, the hospital maintenance crew stood quietly by themselves under the shade of a nearby tree. Next to arrive was myself, Pam's psychologist and closest confidante,

Gloria, and five or six other hospital staff that had come to pay last respects to Pam. The black funeral home hearse carrying the casket that contained Pam's body, followed by the car carrying Pam's family, then arrived. As I remember, there was her mother, father, and a couple of sisters. They emerged from their car and briefly acknowledged those of us in attendance while the funeral director and his assistant removed the simple, cloth-covered, wooden casket from the back of the hearse.

The funeral director placed the casket atop the apparatus that would lower the casket into the prepared gravesite, then gave an almost imperceptible nod to the family, indicating it was time for the service to begin. The family walked up to the side of the casket, one of the sisters carrying a boom box that she perfunctorily positioned on the casket lid. I don't remember exactly what they had to say. I'm sure it was something along the lines of, "We really loved Pam and are going to miss her."

I do remember thinking, *Blah, blah, blah. This is the family who had never visited, never sent a birthday card, never sent a Christmas card, never made one phone call to ask how she was or let her know they gave a damn, and now, in the eleventh hour, they are saying to us all the things Pam wanted and needed to hear from them for years.* I was embarrassed for Pam and erroneously believed this was the final insult to a lifetime of familial abandonment. Like many times before, I was wrong.

After having their eulogistic moment, the family deferred to the "boom box sister." She turned, looked at the casket, and then looked at those of us gathered. She took a dramatic breath and said, "These are two of Pam's favorite songs. If you want to, you can sing along." She then punched the play button on the boom box, turned the volume knob to an unnecessarily high, ear-bleed inducing level, and played and sang along with two songs by obscure rock bands that I am sure Pam never heard of. With that mercifully over, the funeral director came forward, lifted the coffin lid, arranged Pam's head on the pillow, and then stood stoically to the side, allowing us to pay our last respects to her. To say we were shocked would have been gracious. Some staff audibly gasped as they filed past.

I found out later that the sister without the boom box was the person who had niggardly done Pam's makeup and hair. Pam was slathered in makeup that gave the appearance of having been applied with a spatula. On top of a brilliantly white foundation were two perfectly round, golf-ball-sized crimson circles positioned symmetrically above her cheekbones. Her lips were smeared with an equally garish red lipstick, and her hair was oiled and combed in a 1950s pompadour style, giving the impression that Bozo the clown and James Dean had been the inspiration for this fashioning. She was dressed in the cheapest gown in the funeral home's collection. Maybe it was a picture-perfect representation of the family's image of Pam. Maybe I'm being too judgmental. I don't know. I do know that I wouldn't want anyone to have to lie in repose for eternity looking like that.

As I remember it now, though, she did seem at peace.

Several years after the hospital had been shut down, I went back by the old cemetery. But for a rusted metal sign that arched over the padlocked entrance gate, there was no indication that this was a hillside of forgotten souls. There were no tombstones, no flowers, no plaques to immortalize the dead, no crosses, and no way to discern who was buried where. Just a newly mown hillside in the country, enveloped in a perfect and peaceful quiet that can only be found when those who lived with the injustice of an imperfect mind find restoration in death.

Rest in peace, y'all.

Walter

By the time I met Walter, he had already been in the hospital about sixteen years. When I met him, he was in his late sixties or early seventies. He was about six feet tall and would have seemed taller were it not for the slight stoop he had acquired with age. He spoke softly and kindly of and to everyone in a Southern drawl that was charming and disarming. He was a gentleman in every sense of the word. He was polite and deferential to women, always had a smile for everyone, and while not obsessive-compulsive, he was an organizational freak.

As an example, as was the custom for patients who were at the hospital for extended periods of time, Walter was given work therapy, a small job that earned a small amount of money for him to spend at the hospital canteen. Walter's job was to put up the fresh linens and clean clothes in the laundry room on the unit. The patients on other units who had this job mainly just stood around while the PCAs did the actual work of putting the clean laundry on shelves. Walter, on the other hand, made sure he was the only one who touched the clothes and bedding that came on the unit. He arranged it all by size, style, and color. He memorized all of the other patients' clothes sizes and was the one who handed out the clean clothes after the patients had taken showers. I never heard him verbalize any anger, but if one of the other patients or a staff member got into "my laundry room," as he territorially called it, his displeasure was evidenced by unintelligible grumblings and articles of clothing being tossed to his peers, rather than the almost ceremonial presentation he would otherwise have displayed.

I, wrongfully, believed that Walter wouldn't hurt a fly. I was proven wrong twice. On both occasions he believed he was in danger. On both occasions he took care of business. The occasion I witnessed I will relate now. The one I didn't witness was the encounter that brought him to the hospital and will be discussed later.

As I stated, Walter was territorial about his laundry room. It was his domain, period. One day a kid in his early twenties, let's call him Shit For Brains (SFB for short), was transferred to Walter's unit. Each patient room had two beds, so every patient had a roommate. Sadly, the only bed available was the other bed in Walter's room, so SFB moved in. It was an oil and water mixture from the get-go. SFB started immediately to assert himself as the alpha male in the room. He tried to order Walter around and intimidate him in every way he could think of. Walter, being Walter, just took all of SFB's crap in stride, knowing from experience that SFB wouldn't be his roommate for long and "this too shall pass." That was until it was time for SFB to get fresh bedding and clean clothes.

After asking for clean clothes and bedding, SFB was directed to the laundry room, where Walter was the ruler of that domain. SFB strutted into the laundry room and started grabbing clothes and sheets off the shelves without consulting with Walter, as was the custom on that unit. Walter was polite at first: "Can

I help you get your things?"

"Hell no. I don't want an old fucker like you even breathing on my stuff."

"I can get your clothes for you. What is your waist size?"

"What are you, some homo, wanting to know how big my waist is, old man?"

And with that, his next move was almost a fatal move. He took a step back, assumed a fighting stance, made his hands into two fists, and threw a right hook that I am sure he believed would knock the old man on his ass and the fight would be over.

Wrong. This was not Walter's first rodeo. As he saw the swing coming, he took a small step back, allowing SFB's fist to whiff harmlessly past the tip of his nose. With reflexes no one knew he had, Walter then reached out with his right hand, snatched SFB by the throat, and held him at arm's length. With fingers strengthened from a lifetime of milking cows, he began to choke the life out of SFB.

SFB's eyes bugged out, his face turned blue, and his feet dangled as Walter lifted him straight up off the floor.

"Are we through here, son?" Walter calmly asked.

SFB tried to nod his head but was running out of energy and air fast. Walter shook SFB a little and said, "I don't think I heard you. I asked, are we through here?"

At that point, SFB simultaneously pissed and shit his pants, with the overflow spilling out of SFB's pants leg onto the floor below.

"I'll take that as a yes." Walter let go of SFB's throat, causing him to make a one-point landing on his ass in the middle of his own excrement. "Now, clean that mess up, and then go clean yourself up. I'll have some clothes for you when you come back. Now, what size waist do you have?"

End of discussion, end of SFB trying to bully "the old man." From that day forward, SFB gave Walter respect and a lot of space.

Walter had grown up on a ranch in a rural area outside of one of the smallest communities in the state, in one of the least populated counties in the state. To the best anyone could determine, his life was that of a typical rural kid from our state. He divided his time between ranch chores, school, athletics, 4-H, and FFA. Records indicate that he was an excellent student who received several awards for his academic excellence. Upon graduation from high school near the top of his class, he went on to agricultural and mechanical school. It was the first time he had left his rural community and the first time he had ever lived without his family. He studied diesel mechanics, and once again did quite well and received a degree. From there, Walter enlisted in the Army National Guard. There is no record available of his service other than an honorable general discharge a few years later. For reasons he was never able to articulate to me, he later enlisted in the Air Force Reserves. As before, there is no other record other than an honorable general discharge.

By the time he returned to the family ranch, his siblings were married and gone, and his parents had died. Living on the family ranch of a couple of hundred acres all alone, he tended cattle and did the chores he had grown up doing to keep the ranch working. It was just prior to or shortly after his return to the ranch that the symptoms of mental illness began to surface. Because he was living in a very rural area, mental health treatment was never a viable option. His siblings were aware that Walter "just wasn't right," but he never really presented a danger to himself or anyone else, so he was pretty much left alone to be a rancher. As his sister once told me, "He was quietly and harmlessly crazy." His siblings did take guardianship of his finances, but for the most part, Walter was the sole caretaker of the "old home place."

It was when Walter was in his early to late fifties that the event took place that would remove him from the only home he really knew and make him a ward of the state for the rest of his life.

As per Walter's accounting of the event and the police report, here is what happened. As stated above, Walter lived almost literally in the middle of nowhere. His nearest neighbor was about a half mile away, so it was rare that he would ever have any visitors other than his siblings, and they always called well in advance to let him know when they would arrive.

One evening, long after the sun had gone down, two men came up to Walter's front door and started banging on the screen "making one hell of a racket." Walter, not expecting any visitors and having a good, healthy dose of paranoia caused by his mental illness, was scared and wouldn't open the door. When Walter wouldn't open the front door, the two men tried to rip the screen door off its hinges in an attempt to gain entry that was foiled by double deadbolt locks. Not deterred, the two men went around both sides of the farmhouse, banging on windows in an apparent attempt to gain entry through one that might have been unlatched.

While these men were checking the windows,

Walter went to his bedroom, retrieved his twenty-gauge shotgun, and pumped a round into the chamber as he moved from there to the hall. The two men separated, one going back to the front door, the other to the rear of the farmhouse. He heard a noise at the back door, so he crept down the short hall to the kitchen. "Scared shitless," he waited to see what would happen next. It didn't take long for all hell to break loose.

One of the men kicked in the back door that led from the kitchen, where Walter stood, to the backyard. The would-be intruder made it about one step into the kitchen before he was stopped by the flash from the barrel of the shotgun, immediately followed by a chest full of buckshot. He dropped dead in the doorway. His accomplice, hearing the shotgun blast, terminated his attempt at burglary and turned to run off the porch. He made it about halfway to the wooden gate that stood between the house and the dusty gravel road in front of it. Walter had scrambled from the kitchen to the front porch and let another blast rip from the shotgun, hitting but not killing the second would-be intruder.

The wounded man limped back to his car that was parked one mile away, started the engine, and drove it back to town. Once there, he had the balls to contact the police and accused Walter of trying to kill him. His claim was that he and his partner in crime were driving his car, in the middle of the night, in the middle of nowhere, for no discernable reason, in route to a destination undisclosed, when their car became stuck. He further stated that he and his partner tried, unsuccessfully, to dislodge the car from the hole he said they had driven into. They then, supposedly, walked a mile up to Walter's house seeking assistance, or at the very least, to use his phone to call for aid, when they were ambushed, leaving him wounded and his partner dead.

Good story? Yes. Bullshit? Yes.

How do I know the story is bullshit?

First, situated between where the men claimed to have gotten stuck and Walter's farmhouse were two other farmhouses. On that night, both were occupied, with the residents awake and lights ablaze that could easily have been seen from the road. Why didn't the two intruders stop at either one of those houses for assistance, but instead chose to pass them by in favor of Walter's house? No explanation was given.

Second, why did they feel the need to pull the screen door off its hinges and kick in a back door? When I need a cup of sugar from my neighbor and she doesn't answer the door readily, it never crosses my mind to kick the door in, but, apparently to the sheriff, this was acceptable behavior and a plausible excuse.

Third, if two able-bodied men were unable to remove a two-ton automobile from an inextricable defect in the road surface, how then did one man, suffering from a shotgun blast to his back, manage to effortlessly accomplish the task?

The fatality, for obvious reasons, was eventually declared to be justifiable homicide. However, Walter was charged with attempted murder for shooting and wounding the second man as he was fleeing the attempted burglary. Walter was arrested, and because of his attorney's legal gymnastics, was found to be incompetent to stand trial due to mental illness. He was court ordered to the forensic mental hospital for competency restoration.

Normally, after two years of treatment, a patient would be deemed being never able to attain competency and transferred, under court order, to a civil hospital for further treatment. In Walter's case, the judge would not issue an order for transfer to the civil hospital, and thus, he was still at the hospital sixteen years later when I arrived. It has always been my contention that had Walter been found competent to stand trial and had his day in court, he would have been exonerated, be free and back on his ranch today.

Walter had been on my caseload at the hospital for about two years when Dr. Smellyme was hired and assigned to his unit. Dr. Smellyme wanted me to sit in with him as he met with his patients for the first time. We arranged to meet in the treatment team room on Walter's unit early one afternoon to have this meet and greet with the patients. We had seen about three of the long-term, refractory patients on that unit when it was time to see Walter.

"What can you tell me about Walter?" Dr. Smellyme asked as he eased back in his chair and placed his hands behind his head.

"Well, do you want the long version or the *Reader's Digest* version?" I asked, and just for the hell of it, mirrored his posture.

"How long is the long version?"

"Very" I replied.

"Gimme the short one then."

I relaxed into a more natural pose and brought the doctor up to speed with Walter.

"Okay, let's meet him."

I picked up the phone, punched in the number for the nurse's station, and asked to have one of the PCAs bring Walter back. Walter was escorted to the treatment room, where he ambled in with the informal familiarity that sixteen years of the same old shit brings. He sat down across from Dr. Smellyme, and thrust out his hand as his daddy had told him to do upon meeting someone new.

"Hello there, Doc. I'm pleased to meet you finally." Walter's slow, Southern drawl was always a pleasant departure from the manic and/or crazy babblings of most of my other patients. He always made me smile.

Doctor Smellyme responded in kind and began the interview.

"My name is Doctor Smellyme. I'm new to this hospital, and I will be your new doctor. Is that okay with you?"

"That would be just fine with me, Doctor. Smellyme, was that your name?" The doctor nodded. "It's fine with me, Dr. Smellyme. Is that an Indian name? Where is it you are from?" Walter asked pleasantly.

"Why is that important to our relationship? All you really need to be concerned with is that I am your doctor, and you are my patient," Doctor Smellyme shot back, a little too harshly for my taste.

Walter looked a little hurt by the response he got from what he considered to be a benign question.

"I was just trying to be friendly. I didn't mean to upset you, Doctor."

Without acknowledgement, Dr. Smellyme resumed the interview.

"Do you know why you are here?"

After sixteen years, Walter had this answer down pat. He gave his point of view related to his circumstances and politely smiled at the Doc and me.

"You are on some medications and have been so for quite some time. Do you know what you are on?"

Walter sat up a little straighter. "Yessir. One is Welbutrin."

Dr. Smellyme nodded. "Do you know what it is for?"

"Yessir. It's a mood stabilizer."

"Well, not exactly. It's an antidepressant," Dr. Smellyme corrected curtly. "How is it working for you?"

"It's just fine, thank you." Walter replied.

Doctor Smellyme looked at the medication sheet in Walter's chart. "You're also on Crestor. Do you know what that is for?"

"Yessir. It's for cholesterol."

"How is it working for you?"

"It's working just fine."

Looking back down at the medication sheet, Doctor Smellyme asked, "Do you know the last medication you are on?"

"Yessir. I'm on Haldol."

"Do you know what the Haldol is for?"

"Yessir. It's for masturbation, and it's working just fine too, thank you very much."

It was the one and only time I ever saw Dr. Smellyme literally speechless.

Footnote: the wounded intruder sued Walter and his family for damages. They won the suit. Walter has since been released from state custody and is now living in a residential care facility in a small local community.

Some Random Memories of W.

I had to put aside writing about W. until all else was written. W. was my favorite patient of all time.

He was an old, skinny black man who as a young man had killed his brother with a point-blank range shotgun blast. He loved his brother, but the voices in his head told him to do it. If he didn't kill his brother, they were going to kill him. He told me he had no choice.

His family was the most loving and insightful of any I ever dealt with. They understood that W. was very sick and that the "real W." would never have acted that way. His nieces called and asked about Uncle W. monthly. His nieces and sisters would visit when they could and never failed to bring him some kind of treat. Candy mostly, but sometimes W. would ask them, "Please bring me some watermelon. No cantaloupe; I'm not good enough to have any of that. Just some watermelon would be fine."

I don't know what he meant about not being "good enough for cantaloupe," but that was W. He had a small radio that he carried in his pocket and listened to constantly. I think it helped drown out the voices in his head. He constantly needed new batteries, because he would fall asleep with it on. His sisters always complied with his request for more.

I never saw W. lose at a game of dominoes. It was like he was a domino ninja. He knew the "bone" you had before you did. Some said playing W. in a game of dominos was like playing five people at the same time because of all the internal voices he carried and responded to during the game.

W. would occasionally race me down the hall. For an old fart, he was surprisingly speedy. I never won a single race.

W. was a really good dancer and never missed a social event at the hospital.

W. is the only patient who ever thanked me for buying him a cup of coffee.

He loved practical jokes. One day after he played a trick on me, he laughed so hard I was sure he was going to have a heart attack. He grabbed his chest and fell backward into a chair and didn't move ... until I ran up to see if he was okay. He rolled over with a big toothless grin and said "Gottcha."

W. was toothless because one of the biggest SHPOS patients flushed his dentures down the toilet.

I was in the hospital having surgery when W. died. He had been transferred to the same hospital as me, but on a different floor. He was eaten up with cancer. The day before he died, I went down to his room and brought him a Dr. Pepper. He wanted two chili dogs to go with it, but the nurse said they would be too hard for him to digest, so I didn't get them. Looking back, I doubt it would have made much difference either way. I wish I had gotten them for him anyway.

It's fun to think of W. as being restored to wholeness in heaven.

Rest in peace, buddy.

Short Stories

There are many more stories that I could have included in this book. Some were too short, and some were to long. If we ever meet, these are some more stories I will tell you:

- The guy who danced to and sang the song he wrote called, "Girl, Gonna Kill You and Your Family."
- The guy who would give himself a shit shampoo every time he was scheduled to go before the judge.
- The monkey's name was Oscar
- If you weren't such a big guy, I would kick your ass.
- There's a hoe in my dick.
- It needs butter.
- Jackie B.
- The guy who killed his best friend as a practical joke.

www.ingramcontent.com/pod-product-compliance
Lightning Source LLC
Chambersburg PA
CBHW031602040426
42452CB00006B/385